11/03

HOLLY CEFREY

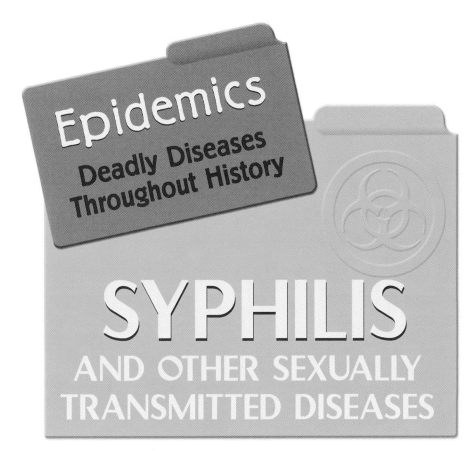
Epidemics
Deadly Diseases
Throughout History

SYPHILIS
AND OTHER SEXUALLY
TRANSMITTED DISEASES

The Rosen Publishing Group, Inc.
New York

To my family

Published in 2002 by The Rosen Publishing Group, Inc.
29 East 21st Street, New York, NY 10010

First Edition

Library of Congress Cataloging-in-Publication Data

Cefrey, Holly.
Syphilis and other sexually transmitted diseases / by Holly Cefrey.—1st ed.
p. cm. — (Epidemics)
Includes bibliographical references and index.
Summary: Traces the history of syphilis and other venereal diseases from the Middle Ages to modern times, discussing their causes, how they are spread, and methods of treatment and prevention.
ISBN 0-8239-3488-8
1. Sexually transmitted diseases—Juvenile literature.
[1. Sexually transmitted diseases.] I. Title. II. Series.
RC200.25 .C44 2002
616.95'1—dc21

2001004610

Cover image: The bacterium *Treponema pallidum*, which causes syphilis.

Manufactured in the United States of America

CONTENTS

President Clinton and Vice President Al Gore help Herman Shaw, 94, a Tuskegee Syphilis Study victim, during a news conference in 1997. Trying to make amends for the shameful experiments, Clinton apologized to the African American men whose syphilis went untreated by government doctors.

INTRODUCTION

My husband is a French soldier. He is far away, fighting in another country in a war against the Spaniards. I have not seen him for nearly two years, and I miss him terribly. I spend most of my time thinking of him and tending to our little house. Occasionally, I meet with the other ladies whose husbands are also away at battle. We read our husbands' letters to each other and try to keep each other strong.

A few months ago, one of the ladies in our group, Emma, received a letter that said her husband was finally coming home from the war. She was very excited that he was coming home. She was also troubled, though, because the letter carried the *disturbing news that her husband had caught an illness for which there was no cure.*

We were all there when he arrived. He couldn't walk, and he did not look well at all. He had lost most of his hair, and his eyes wobbled about in delirious circles. When he did speak, he drifted back and forth between clear sentences and absolute gibberish.

We saw very little of Emma for a couple of months after her husband returned. She mostly stayed at home and tended to her husband. As it turned out, he was not the only soldier who had caught the disease. Other men sick with the illness soon began to return to the village.

Three months after his return from the war, Emma's husband died. The other ladies and I tried our best to comfort Emma and to take care of her. But soon we noticed that Emma looked very ill herself. We feared that she had caught the same disease that killed her husband. Emma steadily grew weaker as the days passed, and a few weeks later she passed away.

Now our entire village is full of sick people. Everywhere I turn, I see someone suffering with the illness. It is being said that the disease is spreading all throughout the country. People have started to call it "the new plague."

I have come to live in fear of the sickness. It affected my sister so that she grew mad and had to be locked away. It killed others silently, with never a peep. Somehow I have managed to avoid falling victim to the sickness. I await the return of my husband. I only pray that I live to see him again.

—Victoria, Paris 1496

The disease that killed Emma and her husband is called syphilis. Syphilis is a serious disease. In the past, syphilis caused large outbreaks of infection. It ravaged the populations of fifteenth- and sixteenth-century Europe.

People lived in great fear of syphilis. The fear was made worse by the fact that the cause of the disease had not yet been discovered. Many doctors living in the 1400s wrongly believed that syphilis was sent to the earth as a punishment from God. It wasn't until the early 1900s that doctors, with the help of modern science, discovered the real cause of syphilis.

Syphilis is still with us today, and although it is now a curable disease, it still infects millions of people in areas across the world. More than twelve million new cases of syphilis occur each year. Many of these cases will prove fatal if left untreated.

1

SYPHILIS AND OTHER SEXUALLY TRANSMITTED DISEASES

Syphilis is caused by bacteria, which are very tiny organisms. Bacteria are so small that they are microscopic. When something is microscopic, it means that it is so small that it can be seen only with the aid of a microscope.

Bacteria are everywhere. They surround us, live on us, and live inside of us. There are many different kinds of bacteria in the world.

The World of Bacteria

In order to survive, bacteria need certain things. They need food to eat, a protective environment, and an opportunity to multiply in number. All of the things that bacteria need to survive can be found on and inside of other organisms—such as plants, animals, and humans. Living organisms that bacteria live on and inside of are called hosts.

Some bacteria are harmless to their hosts, while others can cause disease and death. Some types of harmless bacteria actually help hosts with certain functions of the body, such as digesting food. Harmful bacteria, on the other hand, can cause infection and damage to a host organism. The bacterium that causes syphilis is a harmful bacterium called *Treponema pallidum*.

Treponema Pallidum at Work

Treponema pallidum lives inside the body of its host. The only hosts that *Treponema pallidum* can live inside of are humans. *Treponema pallidum* is a harmful bacterium. To protect itself, the human body responds to *Treponema pallidum* by producing cells to destroy the bacterium. These cells are called antibodies.

When bacteria enter a host, a race is soon on between how fast the bacteria can multiply and how quickly the host's body can produce cells to attack the bacteria. If the bacteria win the race, the host body can be damaged or even destroyed. If the race is won by the host, the bacteria are killed by antibodies, and the symptoms of infection disappear.

- The singular form of bacteria is bacterium.
- A bacterium is a germ.
- Germs are microorganisms which can cause illness.
- Types of germs include bacteria, viruses, protozoa, fungi, and parasites.
- Harmful bacteria can be killed by medicine.
- Harmless bacteria aid in decomposing (breaking down) matter such as wood and dead animals, which returns needed elements to the earth's atmosphere.

In order for *Treponema pallidum* to enter a host, it must be transmitted to that host. Transmission is the spreading of bacteria from one source to another. Bacteria are transmitted to hosts in four main ways.

- Consumption—Bacteria enter a host by traveling along with the food or water that is consumed (eaten or drunk) by a host.

- Air or liquid droplets—Bacteria enter a host through the coughing, breathing, or sneezing of another host. In this case, the bacteria travel along with the water vapor droplets present in the breath of a host.

☣ Vector—Bacteria enter a host through the bite of an insect or animal that is infected by a virus.

☣ Direct physical contact—Bacteria enter a host that comes into direct contact with the bacteria. The bacteria can enter a host in this way through any body opening, including any cut or scratch on the body.

Treponema pallidum bacteria enter a host through direct physical contact. The most common form of direct contact that spreads *Treponema pallidum* is sexual contact. Sexual contact is contact between two or more persons involving various body parts, such as the anus, penis, mouth, or vagina. In some cases, syphilis can also be spread through other body parts if there are cuts or scratches on the skin.

Syphilis—a Sexually Transmitted Disease

Diseases that are spread through sexual contact are called sexually transmitted diseases (STDs). Sexual contact usually involves contact between a man's penis and another person's mouth, vagina, or anus. The vagina is the lower part of the female reproductive organ. The anus is a hole through which wastes exit the body.

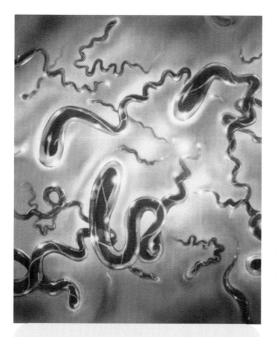

This is a microscopic image of the bacterium Treponema pallidum.

Sexual contact is also defined as vaginal, anal, or oral sex. Vaginal sex involves the vagina, anal sex involves the anus, and oral sex involves the mouth. During discussions about sex, you may also hear the terms "penetration" and "genitals." Penetration means the entering of one body part into another. Genitals, both male and female, are the reproductive sex organs.

Treponema pallidum is shaped like a corkscrew, which enables it to quickly burrow through the tissues of a body. Once inside a body's tissue, the bacterium multiplies itself and spreads throughout the body.

Syphilis causes a single sore to appear near the site of infection, usually around the anus, outer genitals, mouth, vagina, or rectum. According to the Centers for Disease Control and Prevention (CDC), direct contact with this sore is what enables *Treponema pallidum* to spread. The sore itself is called a chancre.

Treponema pallidum isn't spread through contact with toilet seats, swimming pools, hot tubs, bathing tubs, shared clothing, or eating and drinking utensils. The bacteria can be spread, however, from a mother to a baby if the mother is infected at any time during her pregnancy.

Syphilis Infection

Syphilis infection will eventually cause certain symptoms, or signs of illness, to appear. Syphilis symptoms include swollen lymph glands, sore throat, hair loss, headaches, weight loss, sore muscles, and fatigue. Lymph glands are located throughout the body, including areas just under the skin of the neck, arms, and legs. Lymph glands help your body to fight infection and foreign invaders such as bacteria.

Syphilis infection can cause damage to important bodily organs, such as the brain, eyes, heart, and liver. Damage from syphilis infection can also affect the blood vessels, nerves, bones, and joints in a host's body. In the event that syphilis infects the spinal cord, the disease can cause coordination problems and even paralysis.

In rare cases, syphilis infection can lead to insanity. Insanity is a possible symptom of an untreated or neglected syphilis infection. Many years ago, before

1493 to mid 1500s
Syphilis spreads across Europe and Asia from Naples via French soldiers.

1600s
Small local outbreaks occur throughout the Old and New Worlds.

1800s
To prevent the spread of syphilis, public campaigns against sex outside of marriage begin in England, France, and other parts of Europe.

1530
First use of the term "syphilis."

1837
Syphilis is shown to be a disease, not an infection.

1860–1910
Outbreaks occur among European and American military forces.

proper health care and effective treatments for syphilis were available, mental hospitals were filled with patients whose insanity could be linked to severe syphilis infections.

Syphilis that is passed to a newborn baby from an infected mother can cause the infant to die. Even if the baby survives, he or she may suffer from inflamed bones, a swollen liver, jaundice (yellow skin), and a smaller-than-average head. The infection can also lead to brain damage and other serious mental problems.

1905
The *Treponema pallidum* bacterium is discovered.

1913
Syphilis is proven to cause other diseases.

1932
The Tuskegee study begins.

1940s
Outbreaks occur among U.S. military forces.

1960s
Syphilis cases rise across the United States.

1943
Penicillin proves to be an effective cure for syphilis.

1986–1990
Mild outbreaks occur in the southern United States.

1970s
Syphilis cases decrease across the United States.

Other Sexually Transmitted Diseases

There are more than twenty-five different types of STDs. Each STD has its own cause as well as its own symptoms. Many STDs can develop inside a host without the host even knowing that he or she is infected.

According to the American Social Health Association (ASHA), most people infected with STDs have minimal symptoms or no symptoms at all. They feel and appear perfectly healthy. They don't know that they are carrying, and possibly spreading, dangerous and even deadly diseases.

According to the National Institute of Allergy and Infectious Diseases (NIAID), the major STDs are chlamydia, genital herpes, gonorrhea, human papillomavirus (HPV), and acquired immunodeficiency syndrome (AIDS). Each of these STDs can infect both males and females.

Chlamydia

Chlamydia is a bacterial infection of the genital and mouth areas. The bacterium that causes chlamydia is *Chlamydia trachomatis*. Chlamydia is spread through sexual contact.

Genital Herpes

Genital herpes is a disease caused by the viruses of the herpes family. Herpes causes infections of the skin. Bumps, blisters, or sores develop on the genitals, anus, and face of infected persons. Contact with infected skin areas will spread the virus to other people. Herpes can be spread even when sores are not present.

Gonorrhea

Gonorrhea is also known as the clap or drip. It is a bacterial infection of the genitals, anus, or mouth.

Gonorrhea is caused by the bacterium *Neisseria gonorrhoeae*. It is spread through sexual contact of the mouth, anus, and genitals. Gonorrhea can also spread to other parts of the body, such as the eyes.

Human Papillomavirus (HPV)

Human papillomavirus is also called the wart virus. Human papillomavirus is caused by a virus of the papovavirus family. Human papillomavirus is known to cause certain cancers in the reproductive organs. It is spread through sexual contact of the anus, mouth, or genitals.

Acquired Immunodeficiency Syndrome (AIDS)

AIDS is caused by a virus called human immunodeficiency virus, or HIV. HIV damages the body's immune system. The immune system protects the body from harmful invaders, such as bacteria, and from infection. People infected with HIV are less able to fight off infections and diseases. HIV is spread through body fluids such as semen, blood, and genital discharges.

2

THE HISTORY OF SYPHILIS

Syphilis is not a new disease. It has been around for hundreds of years. There is a great debate in the medical, scientific, and historical communities as to when and where syphilis first began to infect humans.

The first written account of syphilis comes from Europe and dates back to 1493. Some researchers believe that syphilis originated in the Americas and was brought back to Europe by ships returning from voyages of exploration. Other historians believe that syphilis existed in Europe prior to 1493, possibly for hundreds of years.

The Origins of Syphilis

During the 1400s, the Spanish Empire was a very powerful force in Europe. Spain was conquering many neighboring lands and sending ships to explore unknown parts of the world. Exploring the world led Spain to many new discoveries and also to new riches.

It has been suggested that Spanish exploration may have been responsible for bringing syphilis to Europe from the recently discovered New World. In the fifteenth century, Europeans called the newly discovered continents of North and South America the New World. Europe, in turn, became known as the Old World.

As Europeans were exploring the New World, they unknowingly introduced many Old World diseases to the Americas. These diseases did not exist in North and South America before the Europeans arrived. Diseases were also brought back to Europe by explorers to the New World. These diseases had not existed in Europe before. Some people believe that syphilis was one of these diseases.

Columbian Theory

The Columbian theory suggests that Christopher Columbus's explorations to and from the New World first introduced syphilis to Europe. The famous French writer and philosopher Voltaire once wrote,

 19

This image shows a wood medicine being processed (right) *and given to a syphilis patient* (left). *In the 1500s, Spanish sailors brought home remedies from the New World to Europe to try to treat syphilis.*

"The first fruit the Spaniards brought from the New World was syphilis." The first documented account of syphilis in Europe took place in Naples during 1493. At that time, the Italian city of Naples was controlled by the Spanish. When the disease began to appear among the population of Naples, it was called the Naples disease.

In 1494, France attacked Naples and tried to take over the city. The soldiers of the French army were recruited from many countries throughout Europe. These countries included England, Hungary, Germany, and Poland. The French invasion ultimately proved to be unsuccessful, and the soldiers of the French army soon returned to their various homelands.

Tragically, many of these soldiers carried the Naples disease back with them to their homelands. As the soldiers returned home, they spread the disease across the whole of Europe. This spreading of disease caused a massive and devastating epidemic of syphilis known as the Great Epidemic.

The Great Epidemic lasted from 1493 well into the 1500s. It is estimated that millions of Europeans died from syphilis infections during this time. By 1512, the epidemic had reached as far as China and Japan.

The disease soon became known as *Morbus Gallicus*, or the French disease or French pox. At different times during the epidemic, the term "great pox" was also used to describe the disease. Historical accounts also used the terms Italian pox, Turkish disease, and Spanish disease to describe syphilis.

Naming Syphilis

The first use of the name syphilis is credited to Girolamo Fracastoro, a physician, astronomer, and poet of Verona. He wrote a poem in 1530 about the disease. In his poem, Dr. Fracastoro created a fictional character named Syphilis. Syphilis is a shepherd who is supposed to be the first victim of the dreaded disease. It would take more than 200 years for the name syphilis to take hold.

Tracing the Roots of Syphilis

Sculptures from the Meso-American era (1500 BC to AD 1500) show humans suffering from symptoms of a disease that appears to be syphilis. Meso-America describes a group of ancient civilizations that reached across North and Central America from modern-day Mexico to Guatemala. These civilizations existed for

This Incan clay figure has pustules indicative of syphilis.

hundreds of years prior to the European discovery of the New World. Findings such as these strongly support the Columbian theory: that syphilis—or a type of syphilis infection—was present in the Americas before it existed in Europe and was brought back to Europe by Spanish explorers.

Although there is strong support for the Columbian theory, other sources suggest that syphilis existed in

Europe well before 1493. Skeletal remains show that syphilis, or some type of syphilis-like disease, had infected the populations of ancient Europe.

If syphilis was present in Europe before 1493, then researchers must explain why syphilis didn't cause any epidemics before this date. One theory proposes that descriptions of syphilis infections are not documented in earlier European writings because the infections were mistaken for other illnesses, such as leprosy.

Another theory suggests that the syphilis bacterium that caused the Great Epidemic was actually a mutated bacterium. Some researchers believe that a milder form of the bacterium was causing mild syphilis infections in Europe for many years prior to the Great Epidemic of 1493. These researchers believe that certain conditions caused the bacterium to change, or mutate, into a more dangerous and faster-spreading bacterium.

The syphilis infections of the Great Epidemic were extremely severe. These infections caused raw, open sores to form on the skin of victims. These sores could eventually grow large enough to destroy the genitals, eyes, lips, nose, throat, and even the bones of those who were infected.

Early Medical Understanding of Syphilis

During the early years of the Great Epidemic, many Europeans thought that syphilis was sent as a direct punishment from God. They believed that God was angry with humans for their sinful ways. They believed that all people would suffer if God became angry.

In 1495, Maximilian, the emperor of the Holy Roman Empire, issued rules against "unchristian" actions. Such actions were thought to anger God, which in turn brought about punishment in the form of disease. People were forbidden from cursing, speaking against God, or gambling.

Physicians during this period in history were not aware of the real causes of disease and had little knowledge of modern medicine. The treatments that these physicians gave to infected patients were often painful, dangerous, and of little or no medical value. In the rare case that the treatments actually helped a person to get better, doctors believed that God had forgiven the patient and had cured him of his disease. If the patient died, it was believed that God had not forgiven him for his sins.

Early Treatments

Early treatments for syphilis included mixtures of herbs, salves, poisonous tonics, and minerals. Often these treatments were designed to purposely cause pain and suffering to the patient. The pain of the treatments was thought to be a necessary step in asking for God's forgiveness.

One brutal treatment was the mercury salve. A salve is an ointment that is rubbed on patients in the hopes that it will cure them. Mercury is a poisonous liquid that comes from the earth. At the time of the Great Epidemic, mercury was already being used on patients who suffered from leprosy. Leprosy is a skin disease that is spread from person to person through direct contact.

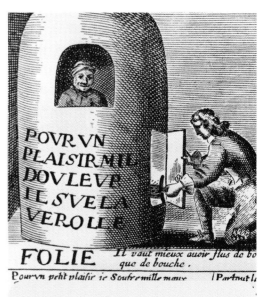

This engraving shows a syphilis patient sitting in a fumigation stove. An attendant puts in fresh fuel to heat the fire.

Infected patients were rubbed with the salve and placed in a hot room near a fire. The treatment lasted a few weeks and was extremely painful as well as poisonous to the patients. Other poisonous substances, such as arsenic, were also used as syphilis treatments. Many patients would die from the treatments rather than from the disease itself.

One treatment that was considered somewhat successful was called guaiacum. The guaiacum treatment was a mixture of various substances along with parts of a tree named guaiacum. In 1519, writer Ulrich Von Hutten published a poem about the guaiacum treatment. He highly praised its powers after having received guaiacum himself. Even though he died of syphilis shortly after publishing the poem, the remedy gained popularity throughout Europe.

Medical Successes

As time passed, doctors learned more about diseases. As the practice of medicine improved and became more scientific, doctors began to realize that diseases were not caused by God being angry. Doctors discovered that the physical activities of people played a major role in the spread of diseases. By the 1700s, doctors were proposing that diseases were caused by small organisms that came into contact with people.

From the sixteenth to nineteenth centuries, doctors proposed that illnesses like syphilis and gonorrhea were infections that came from one main disease, called venereal disease. The word "venereal" comes from the name Venus, the Greek goddess of love. It became apparent to doctors that certain infections, such as syphilis, were spread through sex. It was unknown at the time that these infections, which were grouped together under the name of venereal disease, were actually different diseases with very different causes.

Zoologist Fritz Schaudinn discovered the cause of syphilis.

Understanding Syphilis

In 1837, researcher Philippe Ricord of France showed that syphilis is its own disease and is separate from other venereal infections. Ricord also discovered that syphilis has different stages of symptoms. The discovery of the different stages of syphilis infection enabled doctors to diagnose patients more easily.

In 1932, the United States government began a study to better understand syphilis. It was called the Tuskegee Study of Untreated Syphilis in the Negro Male. It was conducted in Macon County, Alabama.

At the time, more than 30 percent of the male African American inhabitants of Macon County had syphilis. These men were admitted into the Tuskegee study. Rather than receive treatment, however, these men were merely observed by doctors as their syphilis was allowed to run its course.

This was done in hopes of understanding how syphilis progressed to its natural end. It was also done without the patients knowing that they had syphilis. They were purposely misled and told that they had "bad blood." The doctors told the men they would treat their bad blood.

The study lasted for forty years. In 1972, a doctor who left the study alerted the Associated Press. Surprisingly, officials of the study shared all of the details with reporters. The study was then terminated.

In 1905, scientists Fritz Schaudinn and Erich Hoffman discovered the germ that causes syphilis. This breakthrough discovery led doctors in exciting new directions in their search for a cure. In 1906, a scientist named August von Wassermann developed a blood test that could show if a patient had syphilis. The dreaded mystery of syphilis was slowly but surely being solved.

In 1910, Dr. Paul Ehrlich suggested that specific medicines could be made to destroy infections in the body. He called these medicines "magic bullets." Ehrlich soon created Salvarsan, the first effective medicine against syphilis. Three years later, scientist Hideyo Noguchi proved that syphilis could cause other diseases. Noguchi later developed a skin test that could show if a patient had syphilis.

Chemist and bacteriologist Paul Ehrlich established hematology as a field and discovered a remedy for syphilis. He was awarded the Nobel Prize in 1908.

Discovering a Cure

The race to discover a cure for syphilis was on and eventually led doctors to experiment with a medicine called penicillin. Penicillin is an antibiotic. This means that it helps the body to attack foreign invaders, such as bacteria. Penicillin was first used to treat syphilis in 1943 and proved to be a very effective cure.

3

SYPHILIS AND STDS TODAY

As we now have a cure for syphilis, the disease isn't as dangerous on an epidemic scale as it used to be. But syphilis is still a major worldwide health hazard. Syphilis spreads easily and can cause major damage to the body if left untreated.

According to the World Health Organization (WHO), syphilis is the second most deadly sexually transmitted disease. (The most deadly STD is AIDS.) Syphilis infects more than 12 million people each year across the globe. More than 70,000 new cases occur each year in the United States alone. In addition, many cases of syphilis are not reported because many people don't even know that they are infected.

Syphilis Statistics

Studies have been done by organizations such as the CDC to learn whom syphilis infects and when it infects them. These studies have found that syphilis infects Americans of certain regions, ages, and ethnicities more than others. Studies also show that the highest numbers of syphilis cases come from states located in the South. This could be due to a lack of proper STD education and health care in certain areas of that region.

Two-thirds of all Americans infected with syphilis are younger than twenty-five years old. The ASHA believes that this is due to the fact that young people engage more frequently in risky sexual activities than do older people.

Studies also show that syphilis affects ethnic groups very differently. Of the total number of syphilis cases each year, African Americans account for more than 80 percent. Caucasians make up only around 13 percent. Hispanics and other races make up the remaining 7 percent.

The CDC believes that certain problems in society contribute to the high numbers of cases among the African American population. The CDC states that poverty, lack of access to proper health care, and lack of disease education are what make syphilis infections more frequent in African American communities than in other communities.

The Threat of Syphilis

Because syphilis is often mistaken for other diseases, it has been nicknamed "the great imitator." Some of the most common symptoms of syphilis are shared by other diseases. Many people suffering from these symptoms may never suspect that they're infected with syphilis.

To determine whether syphilis is the cause of illness in a person, his or her symptoms must be carefully evaluated. The symptoms of syphilis infection are divided into four distinct stages. Although syphilis infections affect people differently, common syphilis symptoms usually occur at some point in every infection.

Syphilis infections are dangerous partly because early symptoms can be very mild. Many infected people confuse these mild symptoms with those of a cold or the flu. Because they are unaware that they have syphilis, these people are at risk to continue engaging in activities that can spread the disease to other people.

Stages of Infection

There are four stages of syphilis infection. These stages are primary, secondary, latent, and late. People with syphilis can transmit the disease to others only during the primary and secondary stages. People in the latent or late stages of syphilis are not considered contagious.

Primary Infection

The first symptom of a syphilis infection is the appearance of the chancre. The chancre appears anywhere from ten to ninety days after syphilis bacteria have been transmitted to a person. The CDC estimates that the average time for a chancre to appear is twenty-one days.

The chancre most often appears on the outside of the body, in areas such as the genitals and the mouth or lips. It can also appear on the inside of the body in a location such as the inner genitals or anus. The chancre is easy to miss because it's often small and painless.

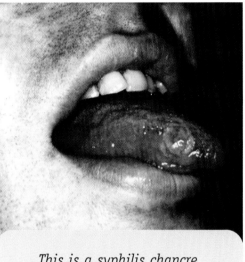

This is a syphilis chancre on the tongue.

After the chancre has made its appearance, it remains on the body for anywhere from one to five weeks. It will disappear after this time, regardless of whether the infected person has received treatment or not. In addition to the chancre, swollen lymph glands are another common symptom of a primary stage syphilis infection.

Secondary Infection

During the secondary stage of a syphilis infection, skin rashes appear. These rashes often become visible three to six weeks after the chancre first appears. The rashes can occur on any part of the body or even cover the entire body.

The most common type of rash causes brownish sores that are about the size of a penny. This type

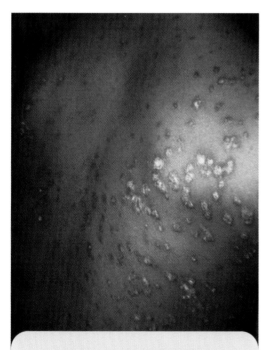

Syphilis pustules often appear on the back.

of rash usually doesn't itch. It commonly occurs on the palms of the hands and soles of the feet.

The rash may also appear in the form of a heat rash or as a bad case of acne. In addition, small, moist warts sometimes develop in the groin area. This kind of rash may also develop in the mouth, appearing as white patches. Rashes of pus-filled sores can also occur on various parts of the body.

Syphilis bacteria are present in these sores and rash spots. This means that the rash itself is just as contagious as the original chancre. At this stage, any contact—sexual or otherwise—between these sores and another person may transmit the disease to that person. Just as the chancre will disappear with or without treatment, the rash may disappear as well. The second stage rash usually disappears after a few weeks.

A person in the second stage of infection may also suffer from fever, headache, and a sore throat. Patchy hair loss and swollen lymph glands are other second stage symptoms. People in the second stage of infection have also experienced weight loss, bodyaches, and exhaustion. These symptoms may appear and disappear repeatedly, sometimes for periods as long as one to two years.

If the infection is left untreated, it may go on to affect the brain and nervous system. Infections of the brain and nervous system can lead to serious, life threatening illness. Symptoms of brain and nervous system infections include fever, sensitivity to light and sound, and stiff neck muscles. The infection may cause difficulties in moving and the ability to think clearly.

Latent Infection

"Latent" means hidden. For syphilis, this means that the disease is present but that no symptoms are being experienced. The latent stage is a period where second stage symptoms seem to have disappeared. During the latent stage, an infected person is no longer able to spread syphilis to others. A person in the latent stage often has no symptoms of infection.

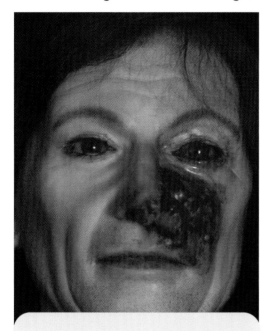

Syphilis can be disfiguring.

Late Infection

NIAID estimates that 30 percent of all syphilis infections develop into the more serious late stage, rather than the latent stage. Late infection has the most serious symptoms. A person in the late stage is no longer contagious, but new suffering begins as bacteria attack the vital organs of the body. Damage occurs mainly to the bones, bone joints, brain, eyes, heart, and nervous system.

People with a late stage infection may suffer in this stage for years. The infection can cause blindness, the inability to control muscles, numbness, and mental instability. The infection also causes heart disease and pain in the stomach. Infection of the late stage is often serious enough to cause death.

Syphilis in Pregnant Women

Pregnant women can pass syphilis along to their babies. Around half of all infected mothers will pass syphilis to their newborns. According to NIAID, about 20 percent of all babies born with a syphilis infection will die at birth.

Newly infected babies suffer from skin sores, rashes, swollen liver and spleen, yellow skin, blood problems, and fever. Children and teens who were infected as babies may suffer from late stage infection. This may harm their bones, brain, eyes, ears, and teeth.

STDs Today

According to WHO, there are more than 333 million cases of STDs in the world each year. STDs are a common health threat even in countries where good health care is available. The CDC estimates that there are more than 15 million cases of STDs in the United States alone.

Teenagers are especially at risk for STDs. One out of every four teenagers who is sexually active will develop an STD. Teenagers are at high risk for infection because many teens explore sex and sexuality before being taught about all the risks involved.

Over the past few decades, teenagers have become sexually active at younger and younger ages. In addition, people are remaining single longer. Divorce is also more common. All of these elements can lead to a higher level of sexual activity with multiple partners. Sexual activity with multiple partners is a major factor in the spread of STDs.

Like syphilis, other STDs can infect someone without that person even knowing it. Even though billions of dollars are spent each year on STD prevention and education, many people unknowingly spread STDs each and every day. Learning about STDs is the first step in reducing the chances of acquiring and spreading them.

Major STDs—What We Know

Organizations such as WHO, NIAID, the CDC, and ASHA research and keep track of the many STDs in order to help prevent them from spreading. Following is a list of major STDs, along with statistics and symptoms of each disease.

Dr. Virginia A. Caine, director of the Marion County Health Department in Indianapolis, Indiana, describes the fight against syphilis in the county, which in the 1990s had the greatest number of cases in the United States.

Chlamydia

⊛ Over 89 million new cases occur each year around the world.

⊛ Over four million new cases occur each year in the United States.

⊛ Over half of all people infected with chlamydia don't know that they are infected.

⊛ Symptoms include breathing problems, eye infections, pneumonia, infertility (cannot produce children), irregular genital discharge, burning while urinating, stomach pain, and pain during sex.

⊛ Persons infected with chlamydia are less resistant to HIV infection.

Genital Herpes

⊛ Over 100 million new cases occur worldwide each year.

⊛ Over one million new cases occur each year in the United States.

⊛ Symptoms include painful sores in the anal, genital, and mouth areas; flulike symptoms, such as fever and swollen lymph glands; burning sensations in legs, genitals, and buttocks; and mental retardation and death in infected infants.

⊗ Persons infected with genital herpes are less resistant to HIV infection.

Gonorrhea

⊗ Sixty-two million new cases occur each year worldwide.

⊗ More than 650,000 new cases are reported each year in the United States.

⊗ Symptoms include problems with the nervous system, throat, rectum, and urinary tract; irregular genital discharge; burning while urinating; arthritis; heart problems; infections of the eye, throat, and anus; and infertility.

⊗ Infected persons become less resistant to HIV.

Human Papillomavirus—HPV

⊗ Several million new cases occur around the world each year; many cases go undiagnosed.

⊗ Over five million new cases occur each year in the United States.

⊗ There are over fifty different types of HPV.

⊗ Symptoms include warts on the genitals, anus, hands, and feet.

⊗ HPV causes certain kinds of cancers to develop.

Acquired Immunodeficiency Syndrome—AIDS

⊛ Thirty million new cases occur worldwide each year.

⊛ Over 40,000 new cases are reported each year in the United States.

⊛ Every hour, two people under the age of twenty-five become infected with HIV, the virus that causes AIDS.

⊛ It may take more than ten years to develop AIDS after first being infected with HIV.

⊛ AIDS can make people very susceptible to life-threatening diseases, including cancer.

4

DIAGNOSIS AND RISKS

Sexually transmitted diseases, such as syphilis, caused by bacteria are dangerous, but they are curable. It is important to seek medical help when you think that you may have an STD, or any serious infection. Some people may be worried that they have an STD but are too embarrassed to get medical help. This can be a fatal mistake. STDs are a personal matter, but they aren't anything to be embarrassed about when seeking help. Doctors and nurses help teens and adults with STD infections every day.

You should feel comfortable speaking with your doctor about your health concerns, and this includes asking questions about sex and STDs. If you don't feel comfortable with your doctor, ask to see another one, or speak with a nurse. Your school counselors can also help you with concerns that you have regarding sex, STDs, and your health.

Who Should Get Tested

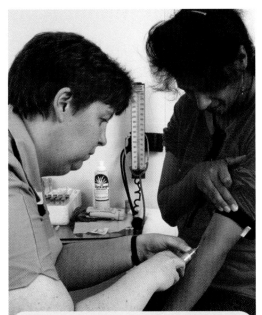

Because pregnant women can pass STDs to their infants, the CDC recommends testing for syphilis and other STDs before giving birth.

People who are having intercourse or casual sexual contact with other people should be tested for STDs. Also, anyone who finds a genital sore or rash, or who is experiencing the symptoms of an STD, should visit a doctor or health clinic.

Pregnant women can pass an STD infection to their children during birth. Sexually transmitted diseases passed on to children are very dangerous and often deadly. Because of this risk, the CDC recommends that pregnant women get tested for syphilis and other STDs before giving birth.

Your Decision

At some point in your life, you may make the decision to become romantically and physically involved with another person. That person may already have a history of physical relationships. It's OK to ask about his or her sexual history. It's also important to ask if he or she was ever diagnosed with an STD. Doing this can save your life.

If you can't talk about STDs with your potential partner, you probably aren't ready to become sexually active. The choice to get involved with someone else involves open communication and honesty. If you have difficulty discussing issues like sexually transmitted diseases, you can see a counselor. He or she can help you become more comfortable discussing STDs.

If your potential partner has had sex before, it's important to ask him or her to get tested for STDs before you become sexually or physically involved. If he or she has been diagnosed with an STD, learn what you can do to stay safe before getting physically or sexually involved with him or her.

Diagnosing Syphilis

The first step that a doctor takes in diagnosing a disease is to speak with the patient about the illness. The doctor will ask about the patient's activities and about any symptoms. Because syphilis has symptoms that are very common to other illnesses, a doctor will most likely rely on tests to diagnose syphilis for sure.

Blood Tests

Blood tests can reveal the presence of antibodies in the blood. Antibodies are special proteins that the body produces to fight infections. The presence of antibodies indicates to doctors that a patient has a disease or infection.

Antibodies are made by the body to attack specific types of infection-causing organisms. If there are syphilis antibodies in the blood, then syphilis infection is also in the body. If you have a syphilis infection, your body will make syphilis antibodies.

Blood tests are safe and inexpensive. Syphilis antibodies will stay in the blood for many years, even if the syphilis infection clears up or disappears. Doctors may order retests to make sure of their diagnosis.

Sore Examination

Another test that doctors can use to diagnose syphilis is called sore sampling. Open sores on the body can be sampled for bacteria. Sampling is a procedure in which a sore is touched with a cotton swab or wooden instrument in order to pick up bacteria. The sample is then examined under a microscope. If the patient has syphilis, the bacteria will be present in the sample.

Hideyo Noguchi proved that syphilis causes many other diseases in patients who are infected.

Hideyo Noguchi was a bacteriologist who devoted much of his life to researching and understanding bacterial diseases. In the course of his studies, Dr. Noguchi developed ways of growing bacteria in artificial environments. This development enabled researchers to study bacteria more effectively.

In 1913, Dr. Noguchi proved that syphilis causes many other diseases in infected patients. He found the *Treponema pallidum* bacteria in the brain of a patient who had died of a disease of the nervous system, and went on to prove that the disease had developed as a result of syphilis infection. Later, he developed a skin test that could indicate if a patient had syphilis.

After his successes with syphilis research, Dr. Noguchi moved to Africa to study yellow fever. Tragically, while in Africa, Dr. Noguchi became infected with yellow fever and died of the disease on May 21, 1928.

STD Signals

There are some general symptoms of many STDs that can indicate the need to see a doctor. If you have had sexual contact with another person, or have exchanged body fluids such as blood with another person, and have any of the following symptoms, visit a doctor or health clinic. Some symptoms of STDs are shared by non-sexually transmitted diseases, so don't automatically assume that you have an STD if you have any of the symptoms.

General STD Symptoms in Females

- Sores, blisters, or warts on or near your genitals, anus, or mouth.

- Itching, strong odor, or discharge coming from your genitals.

- Itching or discharge coming from your anus.

- Burning pain when you urinate.

- Irregular bleeding from vagina other than blood during menstrual periods.

General STD Symptoms in Males

- Sores, bumps, blisters, or warts on or near your genitals, anus, or mouth.

⊛ Itching or discharge coming from your penis.

⊛ Itching or discharge coming from your anus.

⊛ Burning pain when you urinate.

General STD Tests

Anyone who has sex or sexual contact with others should be tested for STDs. Anyone who suspects that they already have an STD should also be tested. Testing involves honest, open communication between you and your doctor or clinic representative.

Testing may involve an examination of your genitals or other parts of your body. Try not to feel embarrassed by examinations. Remember that doctors and nurses are there to figure out what's wrong and to help you get better. There are thousands of teens and adults going through the same thing—you are not alone.

There are a few main tests that are used for diagnosing the various STDs. Tests include urine, blood, and fluid or tissue tests. Tests can be done on both males and females. Doctors may also perform an examination on and inside of the genitals or anus. Open sores caused by infection can also be sampled for the presence of harmful bacteria, viruses, and parasites.

A Fulton County, Georgia, disease investigator steps out of the county's mobile syphilis and HIV testing truck. Traveling investigators screen people for syphilis and HIV as part of a CDC program.

Get Tested

The thought of being infected with an STD can be very frightening. Don't let this discourage you from being tested, however. It is important to remember that most STDs are curable. It is equally important to remember that the few STDs that aren't curable are still treatable. There are medicines that can make living with an incurable STD more tolerable. Researchers are also looking for cures for these STDs each and every day.

Incurable Versus Curable STDs

- ☣ Chlamydia: curable

- ☣ Genital herpes: not curable, but its symptoms are treatable

- ☣ Gonorrhea: curable

- ☣ Human papillomavirus (HPV): not curable, but its symptoms are treatable

- ☣ Acquired immunodeficiency syndrome, AIDS: not curable, but some of its symptoms are treatable

5

TREATMENT AND PREVENTION

According to WHO, the most effective treatment for syphilis infection is penicillin. Penicillin is an antibiotic. Antibiotics are medicines that harm or destroy infection-causing organisms. Penicillin is most often given in injection form. Injection form just means that a syringe, or needle, is used.

Syphilis infection can cause major damage throughout the body. Penicillin cures syphilis, but it doesn't repair the damage caused by syphilis. If syphilis is left untreated, the damage done by the disease can lead to death. Receiving treatment as early as possible can prevent serious damage and disease from developing.

Unlike some other diseases, there is no immunity to syphilis. This means that people who have been cured of syphilis can become infected if they're exposed to the bacteria again.

STD Treatment

There are specific treatments for the various types of STDs. These treatments come in many forms. Common treatments include drug therapy and certain types of surgery. Common surgical procedures include medically freezing or burning infected areas in order to destroy the infection.

It is very important to avoid having sexual contact with other people during any type of STD treatment. Many STDs can be passed to other people during the time that they are being treated. People who are being treated for an STD should inform all past and current sexual partners. This allows others who are at risk to be tested for the STD.

It can take years for a person to discover that he or she is infected with an STD. During that time, the infected person could have had sex or sexual contact with many people, and these people may have also become infected. From the point of diagnosis on, it becomes the responsibility of the infected person to tell past, present, and potential sexual partners about the infection, whether it is cured or not.

The government has begun to make the sharing of STD information with sexual partners a legal obligation as well as a moral one. According to the American Civil Liberties Union, there are now twenty-nine states that

A disease intervention specialist talks with a patient about how to keep from contracting syphilis and other STDs.

have laws that make it illegal for people to knowingly expose their partners to STDs, such as HIV, without telling them.

Prevention

According to NIAID, knowing the facts about STDs is the first step to preventing infection. This will help you to avoid infection and to recognize when someone else is infected. This knowledge can save your life.

All STDs are spread through sexual contact. Sexual contact doesn't just mean sex, it also means kissing and touching another person's genitals. The surest step toward STD prevention is to avoid high-risk sexual contact. High-risk sexual contact includes contact with:

- Someone who is infected with an STD
- Someone you don't know very well
- Someone who isn't open about his or her sexual history
- Someone who is having or has had sexual contact with multiple partners

Safe Sex

Researchers have found that there are activities that can lower a person's chances of developing some STDs. One of these activities includes practicing safe sex rather than unprotected sex.

Having safe sex means using a condom. A condom is a birth control device that prevents pregnancy. It also prevents the exchange of

Using condoms during sexual activities can prevent the spread of STDs.

body fluids that contain some STD-causing organisms. Condoms are available for both males and females. All forms of sex should involve the use of condoms, including vaginal, anal, and oral sex.

It is vital to remember that the use of a condom offers protection only against certain types of STDs. Many STDs, such as genital herpes, can still be spread even when safe sex is practiced.

Still a Killer

Syphilis ranks among the world's most deadly diseases. In the fifteenth and sixteenth centuries, the disease—then known as the new plague or the great pox—sent thousands of suffering victims to their deaths. People lived in terror of this mysterious killer, with little knowledge of how it spread from person to person and who was at risk of becoming infected.

Even though modern medicine has found a cure for the disease, syphilis continues to torment victims across the globe. With more than 12 million new cases of syphilis being reported each year, syphilis continues to be a major worldwide health hazard. If these cases are left untreated, many of them will prove to be fatal.

GLOSSARY

AIDS (acquired immunodeficiency syndrome)
An incurable disease of the human immune system caused by HIV.

antibiotics Medicines that destroy infection-causing organisms such as bacteria.

antibodies Proteins made by the body to fight infections.

chlamydia Curable venereal disease caused by bacteria.

genital herpes Incurable venereal disease caused by a virus.

gonorrhea Curable venereal disease caused by bacteria.

HIV (human immunodeficiency virus) Virus that causes the disease AIDS.

HPV (human papillomavirus)   Incurable venereal disease caused by a virus.

microscope   Tool that makes objects look larger than they really are.

STD (sexually transmitted disease)   Disease that is spread from person to person through sex or sexual contact.

syphilis   Curable venereal disease caused by bacteria.

venereal disease   Any disease that is spread through sexual contact.

FOR MORE INFORMATION

In the United States

American Social Health Association (ASHA)
P.O. Box 13827
Research Triangle Park, NC 27709
(919) 361-8400
Web site: http://www.ashastd.org

National Institute of Allergy and Infectious Disease
　(NIAID)
Building 31, Room 7A-50
31 Center Drive MSC 2520
Bethesda, MD 20892-2520
Web site: http://www.niaid.nih.gov

National Prevention Information Network (CDC)
P.O. Box 6003
Rockville, MD 20849-6003
(800) 458-5231

CDC STD Hotline: (800) 227-8922
Web site: http://www.cdc.gov

Planned Parenthood
(800) 230-PLAN (7526)
Web site: http://www.plannedparenthood.org

World Health Organization—Pan American Office
525 Twenty-third Street NW
Washington, DC 20037
(202) 974-3000
Web site: http://www.who.org

In Canada

Canadian Society for International Health (CSIH)
One Nicholas Street, Suite 1105
Ottawa, ON K1N 7B7
(613) 241-5785
Web site: http://www.csih.org

Health Canada—Bureau of HIV/AIDS, STD, and TB
Brooke Claxton Building
Level 01, 0108B
PL 0900B1, Tunney's Pasture
Ottawa, ON K1A 0K9
Web site: http://www.hc-sc.gc.ca

FOR FURTHER READING

Altman, Linda Jacobs. *Plague and Pestilence: A History of Infectious Disease.* Berkeley Heights, NJ: Enslow Publishers, 1998.

Lamond, Margrete. *Plague and Pestilence: Deadly Diseases That Changed the World.* St. Leonards, Australia: Allen & Unwin, 1997.

Marsh, Carole. *Hot Zones: Diseases, Epidemics, Viruses & Bacteria.* Peachtree City, GA: Gallopade Publishing Group, 1998.

Tant, Carl. *Awesome Infections: The New and Emerging Diseases.* Angleton, TX: Biotech Publishing, 1997.

Yount, Lisa. *Epidemics.* San Diego, CA: Lucent Books–Greenhaven Press, 2000.

INDEX

CREDITS

About the Author

Holly Cefrey is a freelance writer and researcher. She has written a number of books on health related topics. She is a member of the Society of Children's Book Writers and Illustrators, and the Authors Guild.

Photo Credits

Cover and interior chapter photos © Biophoto Associates/Photo Researchers, Inc.; pp. 4, 39, 50, 54, 55 © AP/Wide World Photos; p. 12 © Jim Dowdalls/Science Source; pp. 20, 22, 25 © Bettmann/Corbis; p. 27 © Austrian Archives/Corbis; p. 29 © Baldwin H. Ward & Kathryn C. Ward/Corbis; p. 33 © Custom Medical Stock Photo, Inc.; p. 34 © Lester V. Bergman/Corbis; p. 36 © Yann Arthus Bertrand/Corbis; p. 44 © Reflections Photo Library/Corbis; p. 47 © Science Photo Library.

Series Design

Evelyn Horovicz

Layout

Les Kanturek